RICARD

THE FRENCH

CAFÉ

MARIE-FRANCE BOYER

THE
FRENCH
CAFÉ

PHOTOGRAPHS BY ERIC MORIN

With 211 illustrations, 194 in color

THAMES AND HUDSON

Cafés and places: the **Café du Port**, in th[e]
village of Trentemoult; the **Buvette du P[ont]
Wilson**, on the Rhône, at Lyons; beside [the]
Arcachon yacht-basin; on the shingle at [Mers]
Mers; in the Jardin du Luxembourg, Par[is;]
the terrace of **La Palette Bastille**, Paris;
the **Café de la Fontaine** at Mirabeau;
Chez Magne, in Les Landes; **Le Ronsar[d]**,
Paris, below Sacré-Coeur (*opposite page*[).]

To J.-J. B.

PUBLISHER'S NOTE
Unless otherwise stated, all cafés described in
the text are in Paris.

DESIGNED BY MICHAEL TIGHE

Translated from the French by Jacqueline Taylor

© 1994 Thames and Hudson Ltd, London, and Thames & Hudson SARL Paris

Text © 1994 Marie-France Boyer

Photographs © 1994 Thames & Hudson SARL Paris

First published in the United States of America in 1994 by Thames and Hudson Inc., 500 Fifth Avenue, New York, New York 10110

Reprinted 1996

Library of Congress Catalog Card Number 94-60273

ISBN 0-500-01622-4

Printed and bound in Singapore

Half-title: **Le Brin de Zinc**, Rue Montorgueil, Paris.

Title page: **La Cigale**, Nantes

Contents page: The **Café de Flore** in Paris;

Les Deux Garçons, Aix-en-Provence;

the **Bar Cursichella**, Marseilles;

a terrace under the plane trees in Tanneron in the south of France;

the **Café Costes**, Les Halles, Paris.

CONTENTS

It's three hundred years since the French developed a taste for drinking coffee, this new drink from abroad, and attached its name – *le café* – to an institution which now seems more French than the French, even though coffee was drunk in Arabia some hundreds of years before it came to France. So how would you define a modern café? There are café-restaurants, café-tobacconists, café-bars, café-billiard-rooms. There are cafés selling sandwiches, hot meals, stamps, cigarettes and chewing-gum. All these different functions are reflected in their many different looks. Just one thing these places have in common: they all have to display 'Licence IV', a red-white-and-blue oval card bearing a number which allows its owner to serve alcohol at any time of day. Sometimes, discreetly fixed high on a window, this oval is the only outward sign that inside there is a public place. Behind the

HOME FROM HOME

door, you may find a tiny grocer's shop which doubles as a café, situated on the side of a minor road, and open to all who happen to pass by.

The French do not go into a café only to drink: it may be to make a telephone call, wait for a friend, make a 'pick-up', see and be seen, kill time, work, play, eat, read, shelter from the weather, answer a call of nature, seek out their peers or escape from them. It is one of the few places in our urban civilization where the French can still communicate – or dream of doing so: for there are ever fewer fairs, markets and festival days; the celebrations for Mardi Gras and the Fourteenth of July are not what they used to be. The handful of remaining meeting-places has dwindled away to the Métro and, increasingly these days, the bookshops. Only cafés are left as places of unique privilege and freedom. They are places open to everyone where

anything may happen. For the price of a cup of coffee you can stay as long as you like. In a small village you may find four cafés at one crossroads; sometimes as many as ten at one of the great gateways, the *Portes*, into Paris: you can choose whichever appeals to you, whether it's because of the landlord's personality, the clientèle, the ambience or the décor. On the other hand, cafés in deserted rural areas are now few and far between, though if you are willing to spend the time you can still find many of them in forgotten country regions such as the Perche, the Jura, the Massif Central. The décor of these old country cafés is frugal, but they often create their own atmosphere of romance and poetry with a remarkable economy of means.

In this book, I have decided to concentrate on what is left of the architecture, forms, objects, colours and materials which have given the French café its specific décor. This can range from the *carotte* (the tabac sign, which takes its shape from the packs of chewing tobacco sold in the early days) to the porcelain cup with its gold lines; from the 1950s ashtray to the Art Deco mosaic floor. The waiters themselves are of course a basic element of the décor, especially when they wear the waistcoat of many pockets, one for each denomination of coin, and the apron known as the *rondeau* because it reaches right down to the floor and so goes right around the waist. The waiter is as important to the café as the porter is to the hotel. In Napoleon III's time, the waiters shouted 'Boum!' when they passed on an order, but this call, now, alas, lost to memory, has been replaced today by 'Ça marche!' or 'C'est parti!' often only whispered under their breath as they turn on an elegant pirouette which whirls them off in the direction of the next mission of service. In the French café, today as always, service is a matter of style above all else.

Nearly all the cafés of the seventeenth and eighteenth centuries have disappeared, or are changed beyond recognition save for a few vestigial traces. Sometimes one style has been superimposed on another to create a hybrid look. Survivors of the nineteenth century are far more numerous, and also far more sumptuous, for the café enjoyed a golden age from the Second Empire (1852-70) to the turn of the century. In the country, in the Parisian suburbs, in working-class districts, many cafés have preserved their original décor – dim, friendly places, rich with the patina of age. Apart from these cafés, typical of their kind, there are also the old haunts of famous writers and artists, or the cafés which stand out because of their situation at a busy city crossroads. There are humble little cafés which normally go unnoticed, but which are being listed in increasing numbers by the Monuments Historiques, the body which records buildings and interiors considered worth conserving. On the other hand, there are those cafés whose décor is their major asset. Their survival is in jeopardy, in spite of the determination of some of the new proprietors to restore them; to conserve a style in all its authentic detail demands a great deal of cultural and practical knowledge, and a dedication to lengthy research.

Each period has its style: the bourgeoisie want an imitation of their drawing room, the workers a replica of their parlour. Les Deux Garçons at Aix-en-Provence, with its gilded mouldings of the Consular period, and the little café in the Massif Central, with its cherry-red oilcloth, represent two diametrically opposed images of a whole, rich seam of French history which this book hopes to explore. Not only are they separated by at least two centuries, but also by the gulf between different societies and ways of life.

Page 17: A former posthouse in the Massif Central *(see pages 79-83).*

Pages 18-19: Illustration from an old catalogue of Etablissements A.Berc, suppliers of coffee since 1892.

20

This page, right: Nancy – both the **Grand Café de Foy** and the Café du Commerce with its crystal chandeliers and round-cheeked cherubs look out on the Place Stanislas and 18th-century wrought-iron work by Jean Lamour.

At the end of the seventeenth century, twenty years after the Grand Turk presented Louis XIV with a gift of coffee, the Sicilian Francesco Procopio created a special place for enjoying this new drink, a place sparkling with mirrors, chandeliers, marble and gilding, which elegant society immediately adopted, and which made the traditional, disreputable inns seem old-fashioned. The many cafés which opened in eighteenth-century Paris between the Jeu de Paume and the Comédie-Française, notably in the Palais Royal, remained the preserve of the privileged, the intelligentsia and particularly the political cliques. Cafés of this period were like elegant drawing-rooms with their marble-topped tables and grey, green or cream panelling with touches of gilding, embellished with panels of painted glass, still to be seen at Au Grand Véfour (the former Café de Chartres) at the Palais Royal. In 1780 the publication *Année Littéraire*

THE GOLDEN AGE

pronounced: 'This new architecture seems to be blessed with both wisdom and invention: it is surely singular for a café to show the stamp of true taste.'

In Aix-en-Provence, Les Deux Garçons (the name commemorates the café waiters who bought out the place in the nineteenth century) is the most authentic example of this period. Cézanne liked to sit there drinking peach-based Rinquinquin with his schoolfriend Zola. Then there followed other famous customers – Churchill, Cocteau, Mistinguett, Alain Delon and Jean-Paul Belmondo – it is a compulsory stop even though the locals tend to crowd the place out.

After the Revolution, which swept away many of these décors, fashion shifted in Paris from the Palais Royal to the Grands Boulevards. Under Napoleon III, Haussmann was turning the geography of Paris on its head and the city was amusing itself with

Offenbach and crinolines. Technical advances brought a new look to the French café. The introduction of gas, which meant pipes everywhere, was greeted by a bizarre variety of masking devices such as heavy stucco and coffered ceilings, with large and ever larger panels painted on canvas. New chemical colours made these canvases more durable, and stencilling, while simplifying the designs, made them much cheaper. Stucco imported from Italy, a mixture of chalk, marble and sand with casein, gradually gave way to *carton pierre* (a kind of papier-maché), then to staff (a building material made of plaster and fibre), cheap and easy to work. The Paris Universal Exhibition of 1878 saw a great burgeoning of industrial ceramics, mainly produced by three firms with branches all over France: the Boulenger factory at Choisy-le-Roi, the factory at Sarreguemines and those at Creil and Montereau. The material was bright and easy to maintain and decorators of cafés loved it; huge murals were made of ceramic tiles. This style of decoration continued until the beginning of the First World War even in working-class cafés. Subjects were taken from the paintings of Watteau and Boucher and other eighteenth-century artists. Later Mucha's flower-women and flowing lines triumphed. Many of these schemes have survived, combining Renaissance frames and cabochons with Louis XV garlands and bows in unbelievable complexity. La Cigale in Nantes, dating from 1895, a splendid illustration of this enthusiasm for ornament, is rivalled by the Brasserie des Brotteaux in Lyons. The more modest Cochon à l'Oreille or the Lux Bar in the Rue Lepic favour tableaux of Parisian street life.

Then in contrast to these glossy planes, there are the stucco palaces, those confections of meringue and mirror-glass which still breathe a faint scent of festivity beneath their Versailles-style chandeliers. The Café des Négociants in Lyons dating from 1870, the Bibent in Toulouse also of 1870, the interior of the Café de la Paix in Paris, all are outshone by the supreme Grand Café in Moulins. 'This is not a café, it is a temple, one

Left and below: The **Excelsior**, Nancy, dating from 1911. The painter Grüber, brought here by Daum, designed the stained-glass

ferns in this little masterpiece of the Nancy School. Taken over by Brasseries Flo in 1986, it still retains a feeling of luxury and elegance.

The **Grand Café, Moulins**, dating from 1899. The meat market has moved away from the centre of the town, but the Grand Café – six and a half metres wide, six and a half

metres high and twenty-five metres long – with its amazing Pompadour-style décor by the Italian Galfione, stretches away to infinity beneath a chandelier worthy of Versailles.

26

The **Grand Café, Moulins**. Haunt of René Fallet and his friend Georges Brassens, of Coco Chanel and singer Bobby Lapointe. All campaigning politicians make a stop here. These days it offers brasserie service and organizes Saturday evening concerts in its theatre-like gallery.

has the impression of going into an enchanted palace in the Thousand and One Nights, sheer luxury in art is carried dazzlingly to its extreme limits,' wrote a journalist at the time. The interior of the Castan in Bordeaux (1890), with its monumental grottoes, is so extraordinary as to defy classification. The most successful architects of the day, Luthereau and Duval, understood their clients: 'Art should be present at every festive occasion, offering us splendid settings in which to parade our boredom and our idleness.' What they offered was luxury and make-believe, a setting for the new-rich.

In 1850, with Art Nouveau far in the future, eclecticism haphazardly embraced the great aesthetic styles of the past: the Alhambra, Herculaneum, the Pyramids and Constantinople. Timeless Moorish, Egyptian, neo-Classical or Turkish motifs were ingeniously enshrined in Renaissance or Versailles-style interiors.

Later, with the arrival of the brasseries (the German beerhalls), mirrors, cut-glass and 'style' disappeared, to be replaced by woodwork, brass and padded upholstery. The waitresses, who also obliged with other services, were dressed as Eve in snakeskin at the Brasserie L'Enfer. The French did not take to German taste in decoration, and the Franco-Prussian war of 1870 was looming. Brasserie décor veered first to the 'Alsatian' then to the 'French' style. The Gare de Lyon buffet, by the architect Toudoire, repeats on a vast scale the mannerisms and touches of luxury typical of this time, employing a very French metaphor, an invitation to escape to the umbrella pines of the Côte d'Azur. A more creative period began in 1911 with the Excelsior in Nancy. Antonin Daum designed the *pâte de verre* lights and the chandeliers, Louis Majorelle the furniture, Jacques Grüber the stained glass. They were popularizing a style which until then had been the preserve of private patrons. To the social values of the café were now added its cultural connotations, reaching their fullest development between 1920 and 1970. The café had become a shop-window for a new art of living.

The **Castan**, Bordeaux, looks back with nostalgia to the days when passengers called in to refresh themselves immediately they had left ship. It has kept its sparkling grottoes, its aquariums and the

ceramic sea pictures from the Boulenger works at Choisy-le-Roi. The massive central column shaped like a palm tree, which props up the whole structure, has lost its former splendour.

La Bourgogne, Place des Vosges, Paris. The early morning sun shines into the arcades of the former Place Royale. Women smoke cigars, men walk their labradors. The Bourgogne is a café-tabac and restaurant where you can still find elegant service in the old-fashioned style.

Les Deux Garçons on the Cours Mirabeau, Aix-en-Provence, dates from 1792, the Consular period, with its ochre, roughcast walls and wrought-iron canopy. From this café, shaded by century-old plane trees, countless music-lovers, here for the famous festival, have begun their acquaintance with Provence.

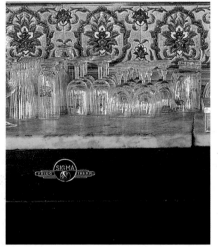

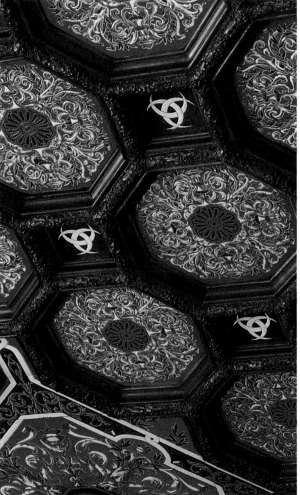

Opposite above: The **Café Parisien**, Marseilles, remembers its past splendour. *Opposite below*: The 18th-century décor of **Les Deux Garçons**, Aix-en-Provence, with its urns, palmettes and Pompeian incense-burners.

Left and far left: The Hôtel de Nantes in Bordeaux used to look out on to the Garonne waterside but now the view is blocked by warehouses. Now a café-restaurant, renamed the **Café de la Belle Epoque**, it has kept its original neo-Renaissance ceramic décor in the Japanese style by J. Vieillard (1865).

Lyons, the **Café des Négociants**.
This elegant café in the Cordeliers
district between the rivers
Rhône and Saône, close to the Place
Bellecour, is now owned by a
famous Lyonnais sportsman. It
serves hot food but has no bar.
Travellers from all over the world,
intellectuals and the local
tradespeople find their way here.

The waiters at the **Café des Négociants** wear a *rondeau*, the traditional apron that reaches to the floor and wraps around the waist. The five-light chandeliers and the eight-branched hatstands are period pieces; with its cream mouldings, leatherette seats, immaculately polished brass, this is an exemplary café.

La Cigale, Nantes. Built in 1895
opposite the theatre, mainly to
provide after-show suppers where
middle-class gentlemen brought
'dancers, lady-friends and actresses',
a century later it is a busy modern
café. The decoration, based on the
symbol of the cicada, which chirps
merrily all summer long, is a
mixture of techniques, styles and
genres. In 1961 Jacques Demy shot
his unforgettable film *Lola* here.

La Cigale. Nantes-born Julien Gracq loves his 'bonbonnière of the Belle Epoque, with its Art Nouveau arabesques and twining creepers in the style of Capiello and Mucha'. The inner room still has its original 1895 cut-flock wallpaper, setting off bevelled mirrors, paintings, mouldings and tiles – Libaudière, Gaucher and Levreau (in 1964 their design earned a listing by the Monuments Historiques), turned to Guimard, Horta and William Morris for inspiration. Scenes of amorous intrigue painted on the ceiling feature the waiter with his perfectly-tied *rondeau (opposite, far right)*.

The workman's café aims to reproduce the atmosphere of a farmhouse, which most town dwellers covet. Here the hearth is replaced by the bar: the nicest ones are usually horseshoe-shaped and can take up the whole room as in the Petit Zinc in Rue Vieille-du-Temple. The walls have turned yellow or brown because of smoke or kitchen steam as at the Tartine in Rue de Rivoli. The seats, traditionally red, are in leatherette, the table-tops in wood rather than marble or cast iron. Mean mirrors share the walls with old photographs. Its appearance is sometimes so modest that you might call it anti-décor: a façade some ten or twelve feet wide painted in brown or imitation wood-grain, easy to maintain; a poorly lit interior; Formica bar in imitation wood, table-tops in imitation marble; often the billiard-table in the back room is the only touch of luxury. In 1853 half of Paris's population were manual workers, many of them unmarried,

THE WORK

sharing lodgings with people from the same part of the country, living frugally, often far from their place of work. Many came from the Massif Central, from the Auvergne or the Aveyron. Before keeping a bistro, they sold water, wood or coal, dragging a cart round the streets; their snug, unpretentious, informal establishments were known as *bougnats*. They sold 'Wine, firewood, coal', and gave the workers food 'just like home-cooking'. The Auvergnats, who worked day and night and saved their pennies, ended up by taking over the whole of the drinks end of the market. For the Auvergnat, the humble zinc-topped counter is only a springboard to the big time. Many Parisian cafés – the Beaubourg, the Costes, the Marly – belong to them. As soon as the train pulls into the Gare de Lyon, the young man from the Auvergne buys the *Auvergnat de Paris*, applies for his first job that same morning, and starts working from eleven to four in the morning, thinking only of home. 'For us, the Auvergne begins at the Porte d'Orléans,' explains a twenty-five-year-old who has been in Paris for only five years and is already the manager of a flourishing establishment.

A whole literary tradition has sprung up around the workman's café: Zola was inspired by it in *L'Assommoir* in 1876, and fifty years later Céline again used the theme of the bistro which 'defiles, numbs, corrupts…' But this 'temptation to children', this 'enemy of frugality and the family' was seen in a different light by Balzac – 'The café is the people's parliament.' In the café, workers find a new dignity, a freedom: it is a place for popular culture and pleasure, where a degree of over-emphasis in manner, a certain number of old jokes and raised voices are allowed, even expected. This freedom, the physical, humorous, delinquent side, is echoed in

ERS' CAFÉ

the names of the drinks – *ballon*, *diabolo*, *perroquet* (bright parrot-green), *côte* – or of the establishments – Jeannette's, Jojo's, the Lorry-Drivers'. Here the drama counts for more than the scenery. The waiter plays the role of the man who sees everything and says nothing: he takes pride in remembering who likes skate with black butter, who likes milk in their coffee. The dim light, the small spaces, the intimacy symbolized by a stove and an old dice-board in pre-war French films, these are the décor of workers' cafés. But above all it is the life, the sense of animation and movement that leaves a lasting impression. Customers of other classes, sensing this charm, begin to move in. Nowadays everyone recognizes, protects and tries to imitate them. Maurice Chevalier summed it up in one of his songs: 'What are they going to look for on the moon, I bet there isn't even a bistro up there.'

*Right:*The **Tout Va Bien,** Lyons, used to be called the Bar de la Lune and was a huge brasserie. Today it is a *cani* – Lyonnais for a small bistro – where the owner, Luce Papaz, with

her cat Vénus, presides over reunions of former regulars.
*Above:***Le Bellecour,** Lyons. Mainly patronized by lawyers, its hybrid décor has its own charm.

Left: The **Comme Chez Soi**, Boulogne. The humble, dark-red façade is covered with countless coats of paint, just like the Café

d'Oujda *(above)* in Ménilmontant in Paris, where the men come after work to play dominoes.

Left: The **Bellevue**, Trentemoult.
A café in the suburbs of Nantes on
the Loire estuary. There is dancing
on Saturdays. The bar was designed
in 1981 by a worker from Bellevue
port, but nobody knows what lover
of tugboats – rarely seen nowadays
– left the model ships and the
magnficient decoration of fretted
cork framing the aquarium .

Opposite: **Le Brin de Zinc,** Rue
Montorgueil, Paris. In this café-
restaurant which dates from 1904
the tin-topped marble counter, star-
patterned floor and engraved glass
windows are typical of the bistros of
Les Halles at the turn of the century.
This is the HQ for the football team
of the Auvergnats of Paris.

Pages 48-51: The **Bar du Clown.** The 1920 tin counter by Nectoux and the ceramic clown décor are original. The new owner, ex-antique dealer Joël Vitte (*right*), fell in love with the café that serves as the 'stage-door canteen' of the Winter Circus and is gradually buying period objects and furniture. Upstairs lodge the clowns Marquis and Charlot, nearby live the Bougliones and a photograph of the late Pépète hangs in the bar.

Le Piston-Pélican, Paris. It is twenty years since this regular customer (*opposite*) first sat down at the curved counter, thirty metres long. The beer is delivered to the café by lorry as it was then.

An ex-actor known as 'the Good Sort', who enjoys good wine, now presides over the workaday plainness of the **Piston-Pélican** which goes back to the pre-war years. The floor, Thonet chairs and engraved glass date from the turn of the century. Against a background of wine vats which held a thousand litres and, like the chandeliers, belong to the forties, there is often a piano accompaniment to the card games. There is a 1960s dice board for the game of '421' – the score closest to 421 wins the game.

54

The **Café de l'Industrie,** Paris. Gérard Le Flem, traveller and film director, owns this little café of the 1880s which he has enlarged by the addition of two enormous rooms opening on to a little indoor garden. It attracts all the young in-crowd of

the Bastille district. The design, recreated on the basis of a few surviving features, combines a certain dreamy exoticism with strict economy of means. Dietrich songs are played in the background.

58

Left: **La Chope des Puces**, Saint-Ouen. In the flea market known as 'Clignancourt', gypsies play guitars behind lace curtains. *Right*: In the minute **Bar Saint-Nicolas**, in Paris, an extremely sedentary clientèle swaps jokes and insults during regular card-playing sessions. The room is dim and smoke-filled enough for the seediest of detective stories. An Alsatian dog hides glumly under the table.

In 1760 the Procope was where the intellectuals met, and the big coffee-houses of the Palais Royal (particularly the Café de Chartres, now the restaurant Au Grand Véfour) became the meeting-places of the Royalists. The Republican Camille Desmoulins, preferred the Café de Foy and Diderot the Café de la Régence, while the warring supporters of the operas of Gluck and Piccinni thronged the Café du Caveau.

Cafés quickly became associated with the philosophers, then with all sorts of new and exciting ideas. Montesquieu said of coffee, the 'revolutionary' drink: 'This beverage sharpens the wits,' and Balzac, who drank it by the pint, was even more enthusiastic: 'It caresses your throat and sets you going. Ideas come crowding in..., the artillery of logic advances, shafts of wit fly through the air.' The first real literary café was the Momus, named after the ancient god of mockery, in Saint-Germain-l'Auxerrois.

ARTISTS' HAUNTS

The Rotonde in the Rue de l'Ecole-de-Médecine, patronized a century later by Baudelaire, next took pride of place, including among its regulars Courbet, who preached the 'right to popular modern painting'. Twenty years later Manet lingered in the Baudequin in the Boulevard des Batignolles, where he would sit and draw for hours on end. 'The first room', he wrote, 'is white and gilt, lined with mirrors full of light.... When you reach the next room, a sort of low-ceilinged crypt, it comes as a shock.' Zola also describes the fascinating meetings of the Batignolles group from which Impressionism would emerge. Manet runs into Monet there, and Whistler and Fantin-Latour. Cézanne comes up from Aix-en-Provence to breathe in the atmosphere: 'On arrival he shook off his jacket with a regular drinker's swing of the hips...ostentatiously adjusted his belt and shook hands all round.'

The **Café de Flore**, in Paris, of
which there is an exact replica in
Japan, is the only French society
café at this century's end. The
ground-floor room is noisier and
smarter, while the first floor is

given over to writing, professional
meetings and to more intimate
conversations. Lunch is served on
paper mats (*page 60*) which, like the
ashtrays, the chairs, the tables and
the wall-lamps, can be bought new.

Pissarro, Renoir and the Orientalists took over in the early 1880s. Degas, for his part, started a migration to the Nouvelle-Athènes in the Place Pigalle; 'A poor, rather provincial café frequented by the bad lot of art,' wrote a critic at the time. This was where Villiers de l'Isle Adam and the Goncourt brothers found him. Cézanne was still there 'with his white linen jacket covered with smears of paint'. At the same time, a year before going into the asylum at Saint-Rémy-de-Provence, Van Gogh painted *The All-Night Café, Arles*; a simple space, lights, a stove, a counter, a billiard table.

In the south of France the 'artists' cafés' still bear touching traces of artists, who it is said, often paid their bills with paintings. That is certainly part of the Picasso legend: in particular, he made many drawings in the 1920s at the Café de Céret to which he was introduced by the Catalan sculptor Manolo. He went back in 1953, delighting the landlady with *Sardane de la Paix*, scribbled with the handle of his son's pen. Juan Gris, Miró and Dali moved back and forth between Céret and Collioure where they frequented the Café des Templiers, a fishermen's café with its bar disguised as a boat, packed with a various and fascinating clientèle. Dufy, Matisse and Malaparte dropped in there. These days Bernard Buffet leaves his canvases at the Café des Arts in Saint-Tropez, already immortalized in the twenties, with its games of *boules* beneath the plane trees, by Charles Camoin, a local painter and friend of the Fauves. But, to come back to Paris, the intellectuals crossed the river to the Left Bank in the 1880s. J.K.Huysmans found his 'port', his 'haven', his 'harbour' at the Caron: 'The walls, partitioned with slender fluted gilt columns, are covered with mirrors. All round the room, worn divans of amaranthine velvet line the walls behind marble-topped tables.' For him, the café was the setting for an armchair voyage: 'Why force my body to shift from place to place when my spirit flies so swiftly?' At the same period Verlaine, Rimbaud and Mallarmé were already arguing at the Deux Magots.

The **Café de Flore**, refined to the last detail, has a terrace – next door to the famous La Hune bookshop – sheltered by one of Paris's few visually pleasing verandahs.

Breakfast with croissants and jam and the newspapers is a cherished ritual at the Flore. The coffee, *l'express,* comes in thick white china cups.

65

Paris: **Les Deux Magots**, on the corner where the Boulevard Saint-Germain meets the Place Saint-Germain-des-Prés, wakes up with the morning sun. Today the manager uses his mobile phone to pass on his orders. The croissants have arrived. The parrot that sings *La vie en rose* comes in with his owners for his *café au lait* nearly every Sunday. The seat where Simone de Beauvoir used to write is marked by a brass plaque under a photograph of the writer *in situ*. The woman who keeps watch over the toilets and telephones in the basement, and sells cigarettes, is another local celebrity.

Far left: **La Closerie des Lilas**, Paris. The meeting place for film-makers and psychoanalysts. The 1920s design includes a splendid Art Deco floor and bar.

Left: The **Bar des Quatre Soeurs**, Bordeaux. There are Napoleon III chairs, bevelled glass, red velvet. As early as 1850 Wagner, whose portrait hangs here, liked to come to this mahogany casket. A caramelized Bordeaux pastry called Cannelé comes with the coffee.

Right: The **Café des Arts,** Saint-Tropez. Charles Camoin and Bernard Buffet were regulars of this pretty café in the heart of the village, where games of *boules* are played under the plane trees.

69

Tavern, inn or posthouse – there have always been places in the countryside where you could drop in for 'a glass of something'. However it was only in 1851, when local prefects were given powers to issue licences, that cafés began to open outside towns and villages. At crossroads, at fairgrounds and close to minor railway stations or coach stops – traffic routes determined their location.

In the country, the licence is often only an extra asset for a small shopkeepers in another line of business: there are countless café-groceries, café-filling stations, café-hairdressers and café-pork butchers scattered across the hills and dales of France. At Norre's in Chenerailles in the *département* of La Creuse in central France, the two rooms look out on the wide square where a cattle market is held twice a year. On those days they are full to bursting with colossal cattle-men and bustling buyers

REALLY RURAL

who gather in noisy groups, for the pleasure of meeting again is as important as the actual trading. Local gossip is bandied about, and this kaleidoscopic spectacle is far more interesting than any background decoration. The place is so crowded that extra tables have to be set in the shop area and right up to the cold store in a kind of back room some two metres square. The waitresses can't cope and the owners have to help out, weaving between the customers, balancing huge trays laden with cold meats. Here, an order for a 'Côte' does not mean that you will be served with a glass of Côte du Rhône wine at nine o'clock in the morning – you can expect a huge steaming pork chop. At a Lille café-hairdresser's the customers will tell you how they have been known to order a glass or two while waiting their turn, only to find themselves two hours later sitting next to the barber, leaning on the counter with a glass in front of them having quite forgotten what they were there for. On the island of Ushant, off the tip of Brittany, card games are played between cups of coffee; people sit in the café watching for the arrival of the mainland ferry, and it's from there that news gets about: 'The plane won't land. It's too foggy tonight, so no newspapers. How are the children going to get back this weekend?'

The landlord of the solitary café deep in the countryside is often a 'political' personality. He is considered, he is consulted, and he may be rudely tumbled from office. In the nineteenth century, parish priests and god-fearing families wanted to abolish cafés, those hotbeds of debauchery where there was dancing. Police commissioners were more inclined to fear the political kind of intoxication: 'Mignon is a rabid left-winger. Give him a licence and you are opening the floodgates to wholesale corruption,' notes a report at the end of the nineties.

You may come across another type of café, hard to find these days: an earth floor, no counter, no running water, with a couple of tables, a fireplace, potted plants and perhaps a decorated sideboard by the stove. You go in and wait as you would in a private house. The lady of the house comes in: you order a coffee, she goes and fetches her own coffee-pot, keeping hot on the kitchen fire, and serves it in glasses. When the regulars come in she just says, 'The usual?'. In the Perche region, south west of Paris, a slate in a café-tobacconist's window reads: 'Red and white maggots – Worms – Bagged compost, medium or large': this is where you buy your angling chart and where you come back in the evening to swap fishermen's tales.

In the Creuse hills they talk of shoots, beats and wild boar; by the third pastis they are grieving for the woodcock that got away. A café-grocery in the depths of the Carentan marshes has such an aged proprietor that it seems quite asleep, but it smells deliciously of *brioche* because the baker's van has just called. From behind her bead

Page 70: A café under the plane trees, symbol of the south of France, in Tanneron, the mimosa capital.

Left: **L'Image,** a café-hotel in Preuilly-sur-Claise, between Indre-et-Loire and Vienne. The parish priest settles his bill at the spanking-new counter, mock-Louis style, standing on the floor designed in mock-*fin-de-siècle* style.

Pages 74-77: Near Loches in Touraine. This room (*previous pages*), with its blue enamel stove, oilcloth and imitation-wood paint under a pale light, looks very like the café in Arles painted by Van Gogh in 1888. In a back room with

a special track (*right*) they play 'La boule de Fort' wearing slippers (*above*). According to the ritual, the loser must 'kiss Fanny's arse', opening the painted window which normally conceals it (*opposite*).

curtain Madame Adrienne calls out to her customers not to forget their bread. She has been reluctant to throw out the azaleas (which will never flower again) because the frills round their pot and the ribbons elaborately entwined in their branches are the latest touch of gracious living. There are still many of these cafés, dozing beneath the eye of an octogenarian owner who is slowing up, along with her cat, and her canary in its cage hanging among the spiderworts and the begonias.

The cafés of northern France are much more lively; they treat games of all kinds with deep seriousness. Some of these games date from the Middle Ages and include a huge variety of registered clubs and societies. At the Café Romain in Lille there are carrier-pigeons in the back store-room where preparations for the racing take place, with a glass of the regional Gueuze beer within easy reach. Pigeon-fanciers organize about forty thousand races in that region alone. Elsewhere, cock-breeders promote cock-fights. Others play dice, bowls, skittles, hockey. At Le Crotoy they do a bicycle 'tour' every evening. They start off playing billiards at Le Siècle, then go half a mile down the road to the Printemps to play cards, then back to Le Siècle for an aperitif. The decoration of such cafés reflects all this wealth of club life. The walls are hung with photos of celebrity friends, of an Alsatian dog or, if it's anywhere near the sea, a boat or two. At Trentemoult where tugs from the mouth of the Loire call in, nimble-fingered pensioners have presented the landlord with model boats which he has hung on the wall next to his lovingly fashioned home-made aquarium. In every one of these isolated, unpretentious and friendly establishments people say, 'See you this evening,' 'See you tomorrow,' and use first names. The landlady shakes hands with everyone. There is no end to the polite formalities. And they keep smiling whatever happens. When these cafés in the hills, in the marshes and on the minor roads are closed down, a whole way of life goes with them.

Pages 79-83: In a remote village in the Massif-Central, a granite floor and vast fireplace, brass and good solid tables. This café, hard to identify at first, hidden as it is behind two petrol-pumps, was a posthouse in the eighteenth century. These days, hunters with their dogs meet here.

83

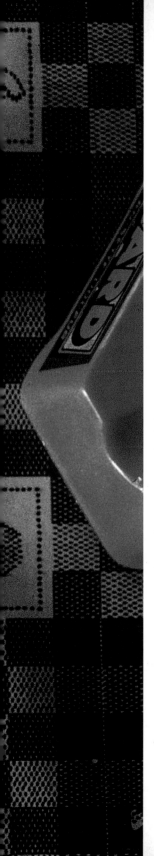

Deep in Limousin country in central France, this establishment, marked only by the modest 'Café-Tabac' sign over the porch of a private house, supplies newspapers, tobacco and sometimes bread. The same regulars turn up every day at eleven; they can wash their hands at the basin outside (*below, far right*). Coffee is served in moulded-glass cups on patterned red oilcloth (*left*). There is no counter or running water in the main room (*top right*): all is done in the kitchen.

Chez Magne, Cap Ferret. Standing at the water's edge, this café-hotel-restaurant-grocery, in fretted wood like all the Arcachon chalets, used to provide meals for woodmen. The grocery (*right*) supplies 'emergency rations' in the form of tinned cassoulet and packet soups. In the summer the smart set swoop in from their sailing-boats to this modest establishment.

86

The café **Chez Magne** (*above right*)
seen from the grocery. Over the
fireplace (*inset*) a photo of the
Arcachon yacht-basin, a bowls

trophy and seats made of wire from
champagne corks. The entrance,
(*below right*) is fifty metres from the
yacht-basin and oyster-beds.

Left above: Having sworn never to drink again, these friends from Tours have opened their own teetotal café opposite the cigarette and newspaper kiosk.

Left below: On the road from Guéret to Aubusson. You would never think you were standing in front of a café . At Eblinghem, in northern France, the sign (*above*) is planted in the kitchen garden.

Touraine. In this grocery-bar on
the outskirts of Loches, they serve
red or white wine, but never
coffee, in a tiny room that holds only
four or five tables. The grocery

section (*above*), the more profitable
part of the business, does a roaring
trade when the supermarket is
closed. The owner complains that
'it isn't like the old days'.

In the twenties cafés stopped looking to the past and abandoned the monumental to try out new ideas. The counter took on a new importance as busy customers no longer had time to sit down. The drawing-room look was out. The big brasseries went French at last with the influence of Art Deco, while the English Arts and Crafts movement (some echoes of which remain at the Cintra in Lyons dating from 1927), De Stijl from Holland and the German Bauhaus had been exerting some influence for over twenty years. In Paris the Dôme, the Sélect, the Closerie des Lilas, the Rotonde, the Café de Flore and the Coupole provided the most striking examples of a revolution in taste: they promoted functional interiors using wood, mosaics, murals by contemporary painters and bracket-lamps in frosted glass. The fashion designer Poiret and Diaghilev's Ballets Russes also exercised their influence, and

STYLE TO STYLE

Le Corbusier tried to impose an 'anti-décor' in opposition to more 'decorative' artists. At the Coupole the pillars were decorated by pupils of Fernand Léger and the floor paved with an immense Cubist design almost as splendid as the one at the Closerie des Lilas. L'Aubette in Strasbourg, now unrecognizable, was created in 1928 by the architect Theo van Doesburg, one of the leaders of the De Stijl movement, together with Jean Arp and his wife, the painter Sophie Taeuber. 'Straight lines, horizontal planes, geometric floor plans, spare functionality.' In this way cafés served to display and popularize new decorative styles. At the Cithea in Rue Oberkampf you can still see the broad bands of plaster in low relief that run through all the rooms in the manner of the Folies-Bergère or the Trocadéro. After the Second World War, plaster became the favoured decorative material for cafés: twisted columns, mirrored frames and seashells

Formica is much in evidence in a small café-tabac in the La Plaine district of Marseilles (*page 94 far left*), and on the tables of a sailors' café in the Baie de Somme with long plywood seats (*page 94 above and below left*). **La Cursichella** (*page 94 above and below right, and this page*), also still has the painted wood-grain of 1870 and the twisted columns of the 1940s. Coffee comes in a very small glass with a very large glass of water (*page 92*).

complement naive murals and indirectly lit ceilings of complex design. The Tournon in Paris and the Cursichella in Marseilles still reflect the charm of this fragile style.

The fifties were marked by a colourful dynamism which made use of painted metal, plastic and plywood, neon lighting and exposed concrete. The great exhibitions of the time – 'Le Beau dans l'utile' (The Beauty of Function) in 1947, 'Le Fer et l'acier dans l'habitation' (Iron and Steel in a Domestic Setting) in 1943, 'Le Plastique' in 1945 – crystallized this new aesthetic. People wanted a 'fridge', and the fridge looked like a juke-box. They wanted wood, a Scandinavian standard of living, 'more human' rounded forms and curves. Before long the plywood and laminates of the benches, chairs and bars had been fused to a film of coloured plastic to create Formica. (The chairs of the Thonet brothers, who used bentwood as early as 1850, have always been associated with café décor.) Leatherette in Mondrian primary colours added to the vibrancy of this style, boldly combining black with electric blue or canary yellow. There was a rapid evolution in seating materials: from polyester to glass-fibre, then moulded plastic in 1970 when 'design' took over the café and developed there – not always to its advantage. The Pigalle in Place Pigalle, student cafés (Le Rouquet and Le Bismuth in Boulevard Saint-Germain) or the Café du Cinéma in Nantes, offer striking examples of 1950s design. Painters borrowing from many styles (imitating perhaps Lurçat, Peynet, Cocteau) have left murals showing cockerels, elves and Columbines, the Jardin du Luxembourg, or silhouettes dancing to a jazz band. To this catalogue must be added the panoramas showing the landscapes of the exiles' nostalgia: Pyrenean peaks or the volcanoes of the Auvergne now cover entire walls. In fact it is the traditional textiles which have lost most through these revolutions, surviving only in the lace curtains of northern cafés and the not very durable seat velvet of the smartest and most expensive places.

The **Cintra, Lyons,** (*above and below far left*). This elegant, well-appointed café-restaurant, all in wood, with neo-Renaissance coffered ceiling and neo-Gothic motifs in brass, was created in 1921 in a style reminiscent of the English Arts and Crafts movement of about twenty years earlier.

Above left: **La Palette,** Paris. The 1920s flat Art Deco motifs on the counter are combined with ceramics that look back to Mucha.

Below left: This market café-tabac of the 1930s on the Place Jean-Jaurès in Marseilles combines melancholy charm, Oriental-type mosaics and murals, and Formica.

Right, and opposite above: the
Bar Parisien, Paris. This café on
one of the teeming Barbès market-
places has managed to keep its
original turn-of-the-century ceramic
decoration framing the big
panoramic picture *Le Roi Boit,*
('The King Doth Drink'), signed
'S.D.V.P. Rue de Paradis', inspired
by a German tavern scene of the
Middle Ages. The counter, although
now covered in Formica, is still
horseshoe-shaped and takes up the
whole room. The façade is all glass.
Opposite below: **Le Tournon**, Paris.
The ceiling and the painted murals
of the children's games in the
Jardin du Luxembourg, are all that
remain of a 1950s decoration .

Page 100: **Le Gallia**, at Cucq,
is on the Le Touquet–Paris road.
Footballers and their supporters
meet in this 50s café, and come here
to buy the sports paper *L'Equipe* .

Pages 101-103: **Le Café du Siècle,**
Le Crotoy. The present owner of

this marvellous café in the heart of
the village chose the colourful
décor. He ordered the laminate
and Formica bar from the local
joiner in 1965. At off-peak hours,
billiard cues and dice share the
place with the school satchels of
children doing their homework.

Opposite: The **Café du Cinéma**,
Nantes. A bentwood chair, mosaics,
leatherette and the 1955 façade
(*below*). This tiny café full of
character is situated just outside
the old Bouffay district.

Right: **Le Pigalle**, Paris.
A handsome 1950s café as it used
to look, with coloured concrete,
painted ironwork, bright ceramics
and an imaginative use of space.
There is a mural of foals, masks and
trees in the style of Ledoux,
(signed 'Lecoq, 1954').

In the seventies French cafés, killed off by the all-conquering American drugstore and despised by their owners who kept on 'up-dating' them, were closed down or transformed into functional spaces, all alike and quite without charm. In the vertical, empty New Towns it is easy to forget that the café could be a very useful space in which to communicate. Intellectuals and hangers-on took refuge in the old dimly lit, traditional corner cafés. In Paris they rediscovered the Bastille district and the Rue de Lappe, home of the Auvergnat cafés. Amid the turmoil of change at Les Halles, Jean-Louis Costes, a former waiter from an Auvergnat café, asked the designer Philippe Starck to create a café with no counter, in the style of the big cafés of the past. The Café Costes opened in the Place des Innocents in 1985 and became a 'cult café'. At that time Starck was designing furniture for the Elysée Palace, remodelling the Museum of

CULT CAFÉS

Decorative Art, collaborating on the Parc de la Villette project and designing furniture and other objects for the mail-order catalogue of Les 3 Suisses. Fired with enthusiasm, he dreamed up a huge, plain interior predominantly verdigris in colour, to celebrate the eighties. He renovated the tables and benches, revived the idea of bevelled mirrors and paid special attention to the basement area – telephones and toilets – neglected since 1920. The effect was austere, the materials chilly. The Berlin Wall still stood, and Starck, nostalgic for Eastern Europe, sought to evoke 'the melancholy buffet of Prague railway station'. The success of this post-modernist romanticism was reflected in the spawning of numerous small 'Starck-type' cafés in the provinces together with cafés in the style of Andrée Putman, the first lady of design, with their contrasting blacks and whites and almost clinical plain greys.

Pages 106, 108-109. **Café Marly**, Paris. Exploding with colour, it was designed in 1994 by Olivier Gagnère and Yves Taralon in the Morny salon within the former

Palais du Louvre. A fabulous location – it looks out on both Pei's pyramid and the Marly courtyard where French 18th-century sculpture is exhibited.

But, above the prefabricated verandahs of other cafés, the painted metal tabac sign is giving way to an ugly lozenge, which, with the green and red rectangle of the PMU (the French betting totalizator), the four blue and red cubes of the National Lottery, the beer advertisements and the green Métro ticket, adds to the graphic chaos. Inside, the billiard room is still full of surprisingly lively activity, but there are new methods of communication: the customers' mobile phones, the waiters' computer.

With the recession, actors, journalists, make-up artists, antique-dealers and musicians have been moved by nostalgia for these places to get behind the counter and to attempt to restore, copy and create replicas of the workers' cafés of the early twentieth century; it is a small sociological phenomenon. Thus the Cochon à l'Oreille, the Clown and particularly the Café de l'Industrie are becoming fashionable haunts.

However, the great event of the 1990s is undoubtedly the Marly. Its owner, Jean-Louis Costes, with his brother Gilbert, also owns the Costes and the Café Beaubourg, keeping up the tradition of the Auvergnat café proprietor. The Marly, signalling a return to the middle-class café of the 1880s with its 'amaranthine velvet' celebrated by Huysmans, looks back to even earlier styles such as you find at Les Deux Garçons with its perfume-burners. Here the reference to the antique comes from the Venetian glass chandeliers and the Pompeian walls 'in Herculaneum earth-colours': these wall decorations, treated with great sophistication, reflect the current taste for good materials and fine workmanship. The place is not without touches of humour, and maintains a certain distance from previous styles: more than anything else, the chic, comfortable Café Marly resembles the Florian in Venice of which Henri de Régnier wrote in 1909: 'These small rooms are so agreeable with their curved seats and their sense of intimacy. One quickly feels at home there...in spite of a faintly old-fashioned air, something agreeably rococo, a little in the style...of our Second Empire.'

Left: **Le Café Costes**, Paris. This big Post-Modern café, a symbol of the 1980s, was designed by Philippe Starck in 1985. Sadly, it has now closed down.

Above: The **Café Beaubourg** was designed by Christian de Portzamparc at the end of the 1980s. Situated opposite the Pompidou Centre, its customers include visitors to the gallery, painters and dealers.

*'The glass of wine has become
the universal ritual of communication.
The bistro is our oasis.'*
Edgar Morin

The author

wishes to thank

B. Saalburg

R. Beaufre

J. Chouty

A. de Condé

C. Cussinet

J. Pinçon

J.-L. Gaillemin

GUIDE

Listed here are a hundred cafés of character in and around
Paris and in the provinces of France, chosen for their décor, location or ambience.
Roman numerals, e.g. (IX), after certain café titles refer to their city district.
(M.H.): this marks those cafés classified or listed on the
Inventory of Monuments Historiques.
Some of the places that appear in the book are not included in the Guide, and
vice-versa. If certain of the isolated rural cafés are to stay as they are, or even to survive,
it would be too much of a risk to send readers in search of them.

PARIS - CAFÉS

LE CAFÉ DE L'EPOQUE (I)
2 Rue du Bouloi. 42 33 40 70. Situated in the
delightful Passage Vero-Dodat in Les Halles.

LE COCHON A L'OREILLE (I)
15 Rue Montmartre. 42 36 07 56. Ceramic
panels illustrating scenes of Les Halles.

LE BRIN DE ZINC (I)
50 Rue Montorgueil. 42 21 10 80. In the
Les Halles district – interesting floor and
counter, engraved glass of 1900. Renovated.

LE GUTENBERG (I)
29 Rue Coquillière. 45 08 11 11. A few yards
from the Place des Victoires, centre of the
fashion trade. 'Modernist' painted panels
under glass.

ROYAL BAR (II)
143 Rue Saint-Denis. Italian provincial style
fin-de-siècle mosaics, 1950s juke box and
somewhat dubious backroom.

LA BOURGOGNE (III)
19 Place des Vosges. 42 78 44 64. Terraces under
the arcades of one of Paris's most beautiful squares.

L'ALLEE THORIGNY (III)
2 Place Thorigny.
1920s bar, contemporary atmosphere and near
the Picasso Museum.

BRASSERIE LES DEUX PALAIS (IV)
3 Boulevard du Palais. 43 54 20 86.
Hybrid décor of 19th-century mirrors
and 'drugstore'; lawyers' favourite haunt.

LE PETIT FER A CHEVAL (IV)
30 Rue Vieille-du-Temple. 42 72 47 47.
In the Marais district. Remarkable for
its horseshoe counter, inner room and
toilets in bolted metal submarine-style.

LA TARTINE (IV)
24 Rue de Rivoli. 42 72 76 85.
An old Auvergnat café, totally authentic.
Intellectuals, now as always. A cult café.

LE BEAUBOURG (IV)
43 Rue Saint-Merri. 48 87 63 96. Opposite
the Pompidou Centre, a meeting-place for
curators and restorers. 1980s décor, clean and
uncluttered, by Christian de Portzamparc.

LE MARLY (IV)
93 Rue de Rivoli. 49 26 06 60. In the tradition
of the big, smart cafés, this is set to be the cult
café of the late 20th century. Sumptuously
decorated in 1994 by Olivier Gagnère and
Yves Taralon, facing the Louvre pyramid and
backing on to the Cour Marly.

CAFÉ MAURE DE LA MOSQUEE (V)
39 Avenue Geoffroy-Saint-Hilaire. 43 31 18 14.
Gorgeous decoration in the style of Pierre Loti,
mint tea and gazelle horns.

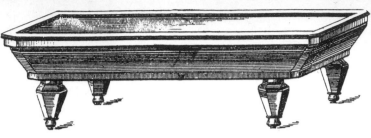

CAFÉ DE FLORE (VI)
172 Boulevard Saint-Germain. 45 48 55 26.
1925 décor, wonderful location, famous as a
haunt of the literary and fashionable, a great
place for meeting friends. Cult café. (M.H.)

LES DEUX MAGOTS (VI)
6 Place Saint-Germain-des-Prés. 45 48 55 25. For
its mock-Louis XIV décor, its light and its view of
the church of Saint-Germain.

LE SELECT (VI)
99 Boulevard du Montparnasse. 45 48 38 24.
A historic café. 1920s interior, Art Deco mouldings.

LE BONAPARTE (VI)
42 Rue Bonaparte. 43 26 42 81.
A good place to meet. View of the church of Saint-
Germain-des-Prés.

LE CAFÉ DE LA MAIRIE (VI)
8 Place Saint-Sulpice. 43 26 67 82. Has a shady
terrace overlooking the Place Saint-Sulpice with its
church and fountain.

LA BRULERIE DE L'ODEON (VI)
6 Rue de Crébillon. 43 26 39 32.
Once a colonial store and coffee-roasting shop and
has kept its fragrant, old-fashioned interior.

LA PALETTE (VI)
43 Rue de Seine. 43 26 68 15. Smoky back room
of about 1900. A 'local' for students and artists.
(M.H.)

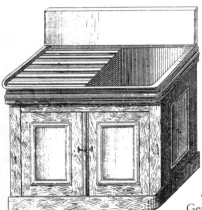

**AU SAUVIGNON
(VII)**
80 Rue des Saints-Pères.
45 48 49 02. Early 20th-
century counter, and
caricatures of the
Auvergnat family that
owns the establishment.

LE ROUQUET (VII)
188 Boulevard Saint-
Germain. 45 48 06 93.
Unpretentious 1950s style
on the Boulevard Saint-
Germain, student atmosphere.

LE TOURNON (VII)
18 Rue de Tournon. 43 26 61 16. Good view of the
Senate, interesting ceiling, post-war murals of the
Jardin du Luxembourg.

CAFÉ DE LA PAIX (IX)
12 Boulevard des Capucines, Place de l'Opéra. 40 07
30 10. Imposing Louis XVI interior, ceiling by
Garnier, Doric columns.

AUX CUVES D'ARGENT (XI)
104 Rue Saint-Maur. 43 57 16 02. Unique décor,
working-class atmosphere.

CAFÉ-CHARBON (XI)
109 Rue Oberkampf. Old-fashioned décor,
discreetly and cleverly revamped.

LE CITHEA (XI)
114 Rue Oberkampf. 40 21 70 95. 1920s moulded
reliefs, billiard room, renovated fittings.

BAR DU CLOWN (XI)
114 rue Amelot. 43 55 87 35. Next door to the
Cirque d'Hiver. Ceramics. Tries to keep its special
charm as a club for circus-lovers.

LA ROTONDE-BASTILLE (XI)
17 Rue de la Roquette. 47 00 68 93. The best place
to meet near the Bastille. Humming with life.

LA RENAISSANCE (XI)
87 Rue de la Roquette. Low lights, traditional
ambience, interesting floor and bar, local clientèle.

LE BLUE BILLARD (XI)
111 Rue Saint-Maur. 43 55 87 21. Contemporary
décor. Billiard-rooms at the back.

CAFÉ DE L'INDUSTRIE (XI)
12 Rue Sedaine. This remodelling of a dim,
traditional workers' café attracts all the young
trendies.

LE BISTROT DU PEINTRE (XI)
116 Avenue Ledru-Rollin. 47 00 34 39. Modern Style (renovated), tiled decoration. (M.H.)

LE LIMONAIRE (XII)
88 Rue de Charenton. 43 43 49 14. Sombre, traditional 1900s style. Well restored counter, floor and seats.

LES MOUSQUETAIRES (XIV)
77 Avenue du Maine. Contemporary décor. The billiard room has an old-fashioned dome.

CHEZ WALCZACK (XV)
75 Rue de Brancion. 48 28 61 00. Dim, traditional, covered with photos of the boxing fraternity. Nostalgic.

LE RONSARD (XVIII)
13 Place Saint-Pierre. 46 06 03 38. Close to the Saint-Pierre market where you buy 'seconds' in fabrics. The terrace looks out to the Sacré-Coeur.

LE BAR PARISIEN (XVIII)
36 Boulevard d'Ornano. Ceramic decoration, 'The King Doth Drink', depicting a Flemish festival. Medieval style. Workers' café.

LUX BAR (XVIII)
12 Rue Lepic. 46 06 05 15. 1900 tiled decoration showing life in the streets of Paris. Renovated in a mixture of styles. Workers' café.

LE PIGALLE (XVIII)
22 Boulevard de Clichy. 46 06 72 90. Now called Chao Ba Café, with the 1950s-style décor partially obscured. (M.H.)

LE BOUGNAT (XVIII)
39 Rue Durantin. 42 62 15 82. Snug dimensions, memories of the coal-and-wood-sellers' cafés of the old days.

LE PISTON-PELICAN (XX)
15 Rue de Bagnolet. 43 70 35 00. Real workers' café which has a wonderful, totally authentic original décor.

CAFÉ-BOIS-CHARBONS (XX)
49 Rue Orfila. 46 36 73 60. Old 'coal merchant's' facade and homely atmosphere, with a log-fire in the hearth.

SAINT-OUEN *(Northern suburb of Paris)*

CHEZ LOUISETTE
130 Avenue Michelet. 40 12 10 14. Situated right inside the Clignancourt flea market in the Marché Vernaison, working-class style; neo-realist singers in the Piaf tradition (Saturday-Sunday-Monday).

LA CHOPE DES PUCES
122 Rue des Rosiers. 40 11 02 49. Working-class ambience, in the heart of the fleamarket. Gipsy guitarists (Saturday-Sunday-Monday).

PARIS - BRASSERIES
Cafés within the great brasseries decorated in brass and wood, ceramics and potted palms: full service for the ideal breakfast.

CAFÉ BRASSERIE DU GRAND COLBERT (II)
2–4 Rue Vivienne. 42 86 87 88. Between the Palais Royal and the Bourse.

CAFÉ BRASSERIE BALZAR (V)
49 Rue des Ecoles. 43 54 13 67. Latin Quarter, close to the Sorbonne.

CAFÉ BRASSERIE DE LA CLOSERIE DES LILAS (VI)
171 Boulevard du Montparnasse. 43 26 70 50. The district beloved of artists and Hemingway. Splendid floor.

CAFÉ BRASSERIE LIPP (VI)
151 Boulevard Saint-Germain. 45 48 53 91.
Saint-Germain-des-Prés, opposite the
Café de Flore.

CAFÉ BRASSERIE MOLLARD (VIII)
113 Rue Saint-Lazare. 43 87 50 22.
Opposite the Gare Saint-Lazare,
1900s tiles.

CAFÉ TERMINUS NORD (X)
23 Rue de Dunkerque. 42 85 05 15.
Opposite the Gare du Nord, magnificent floor.
Perfect décor.

CAFÉ DU TRAIN BLEU (XII)
Place Louis-Armand. 43 43 09 06.
Exuberant decoration, huge murals of the
Gare de Lyon.

CAFÉ BRASSERIE DE LA COUPOLE (XIV)
102 Boulevard du Montparnasse. 43 20 14 20.
Exceptional floor, 1925 pillars, well restored.

AIX-EN-PROVENCE
(Bouches-du-Rhône)

LES DEUX GARCONS
Cours Mirabeau. 42 26 00 51.
The gold and ivory décor goes
back to 1792, an exceptionally
elegant interior. (M.H.)

BANDOL - *(Var)*

CAVE BANDOLAISE
14 Rue de la République.
94 29 48 71. Excellent
choice of wines, arcane
atmosphere. This is where
they celebrate the vintage.

LE NARVAL
2 Place de la Liberté.
94 29 40 16. This is a typical
café terrace of the Côte d'Azur,
where you can sit out on rattan furniture
under palm-trees by the sea.

BORDEAUX - *(Gironde)*

LA BELLE EPOQUE
2 Allée d'Orléans, Place des
Quinconces. 1880s décor. Not such a
desirable meeting-place any more.

LE CAFÉ DU MUSEE CAPC
Entrepôts Lainé, 7 Rue Ferrière.
On the roof of a great modern
museum in the Lainé Warehouses
designed by Andrée Putman.

BAR DES 4 SOEURS
6 Cours du 30 Juillet. 1850s chocolate-box décor
beloved of Wagner.

LE CASTAN
2 Quai de la Douane. Preposterous 1890s grotto,
lacy metal canopy. Workers' café.

LE GAULOIS
3 Place des Victoires. Lacy metal
canopy, interior in a mixture of styles,
much loved by students.

AVIATIC CAFÉ
41 Rue des Augustins. 56 94 74 00.
American cinema decorations, five
television sets, switched on.

CAFÉ DES ARTS
Cours Victor Hugo. Unpretentious
post-war décor, Thonet seats,
wrought ironwork, tiles. Nostalgic.

LE BISTROT DES QUINCONCES
4 Place des Quinconces. Good
rendezvous. Well-appointed, chic and
trendy. Bevelled windows, traces of
earlier decorative schemes.

CAP FERRET - *(Gironde)*

CHEZ MAGNE
Hotel de la Plage, L'Herbe, Cap Ferret. 56 60 50 15.
Part of a hotel-grocery-restaurant in fretted
woodwork of the 1880s, thirty yards from the sea,
on the Arcachon dockside.

LE PINASSE CAFÉ
2 bis Avenue de l'Océan.
Views of the sea, delightful
decorations.

CERET
(Pyrénées-Orientales)

LE GRAND CAFÉ
1 Boulevard Maréchal Joffre.
68 87 02 85. Interesting
paintings, past connections
with Picasso and his friends.

COLLIOURE - *(Pyrénées-Orientales)*

LE CAFÉ DES TEMPLIERS
Quai de l'Amirauté. 68 98 31 10. Fishing-boat
bar, where painters, fishermen and writers have
always rubbed shoulders.

HONFLEUR - *(Calvados)*

CAFÉ DES ARTISTES
For its atmosphere, history and paintings.

LA ROCHELLE - *(Charente-Maritime)*

CAFÉ DE LA PAIX
56 Rue Chaudrier. 46 41 39 79. Napoleon III
décor, 1930s painted ceilings. Simenon (creator
of Maigret) used to come here. (M.H.)

LE CROTOY - *(Somme)*

LE SIECLE
5 Place due Monument aux Morts. Original 1965
decoration. Workers' café.

LILLE - *(Nord)*

LES BRASSEURS
22 Place de la Gare. 20 06 46 25. New beer-vats, a
saloon atmosphere.

LYONS - *(Rhône)*

CAFÉ DES NEGOCIANTS (II)
1 Place Francisque Regaud. Lovely 1870s décor.
The rendezvous of the Cordeliers district.

BAR DE L'HOTEL-DIEU (II)
4 Rue Turpin. 78 42 11 98. Tiled mural.
Unpretentious.

CAFÉ BELLECOUR (II)
33 Place Bellecour. Mixed decorative scheme,
overlooks Lyons's prettiest square.

LE CINTRA (II)
42 Rue de la Bourse. 78 42 54 08. Smart, plushy,
neo-Gothic plus Arts and Crafts décor (especially
the restaurant).

BUVETTE DU PONT WILSON (III)
15 Quai Augagneur. Log-cabin architecture, view
over the Rhône.

CAFÉ DU RHONE (III)
23 Quai Augagneur. Very small, perfect in its way.
Original ceramic decorations, attractive woodwork,
stove in the middle of the room. (M.H.)

**CAFÉ-RESTAURANT DE
FOURVIERE** (V)
9 Place de Fourvière. 78 25 21 15.
This café has a panoramic view of the
town, and is close to the extraordinary
basilica and a kitsch statue.

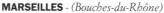

MARSEILLES - *(Bouches-du-Rhône)*

CHEZ GERMAIN
Restaurant Le Château
Calanque de Sormiou. 91 25
08 69. Isolated location,
exceptional view over the
Mediterranean.

LE NEW-YORK (I)
33 Quai des Belges. 91 33
91 79. Meet your friends here
at the old port; chic café-
brasserie style.

BAR CURSICHELLA (II)
59 Boulevard des Dames. 1940s-revival decoration, close to where the ferries sail for Corsica.

CAFÉ PARISIEN (II)
1 Place Sadi-Carnot. Original 1903 décor, oddly combined with Philippe Starck furniture. Restored.

LES FLOTS BLEUS (V)
82 Corniche Kennedy. Sea view, 50s architecture.

BAR DU VALLON (VII)
Vallon des Auffes, 169 Corniche Kennedy. Overlooks a fishing port, lively and picturesque.

BAR DE LA MARINE (VII)
15 Quai de Rive-Neuve. 91 54 95 42. Overlooks the old port, naive modern decorations.

MERS-LES-BAINS - *(Somme)*

LES MOUETTES
Place Eugène Dabit. 35 86 30 38. Right on the shingle at the foot of the cliffs. View of the sea and Le Tréport.

METZ - *(Moselle)*

FLO-METZ
87 85 94 95. Café in the brasserie of the same name.

MIRABEAU
(Alpes-de-Haute-Provence)

CAFÉ DE LA FONTAINE
Place de la Fontaine. The terrace, under the plane trees, beside the fountain, could be from a film by Pagnol.

MOULINS - *(Allier)*

LE GRAND CAFÉ
49 Place d'Allier. 70 44 00 05. Outstanding 1899 rococo decoration, newly painted in sea-green. (M.H.)

CAFÉ DE LA POSTE
10 Rue Amelot. 1900 façade, delightful interior.

NANCY
(Meurthe-et-Moselle)

EXCELSIOR
50 Rue Henri Poincaré. 83 35 24 57. Outstanding School-of-Nancy decorations (1911) designed by Majorelle, Daum and Grüber (M.H.)

L'INSTITUT
102 Grand Rue. Located in the old town, bar with brass fittings, turn-of-the-century decorations. Students gather here.

CAFÉ DU COMMERCE
Place Stanislas. 33 35 52 62. Go there for the crystal chandeliers and the view over the famous Place Stanislas with its 18th-century wrought-iron work by Jean Lamour.

NANTES - *(Loire-Atlantique)*

LA CIGALE
4 Place Graslin. 51 84 94 94. Crazy 1895 décor, still intact, cheerful after-theatre ambience. (M.H.)

LE LOUIS XIV
94 Rue Maréchal-Joffre. 1950s décor, Formica, plywood and enormous black-and-white photographs.

LE CAFÉ DU CINEMA
4 Rue des Carmélites. Unpretentious 1950s décor, close to the old district of the Bouffay and near the cathedral.

LE CAFÉ BELLEVUE
20 Quai Marcel-Boissard, Trentemoult, in the Nantes suburbs. Naive tug-boat decorations, view of the Loire estuary.

OLLIOULES - *(Var)*

BAR TROTOBOIS
Place de la Mairie. Terrace with palm-trees
overlooking the Provençal market on the square.

RHEIMS - *(Marne)*

CAFÉ DU PALAIS
14 Place Mirron-Herrick. 26 47 52 54. Arty
atmosphere and cheerfully crazy early-1900s décor.
Where the local intelligentsia meet.

SAINT-REMY-DE-PROVENCE - *(Bouches-du-Rhône)*

CAFÉ DES ARTS
30 Boulevard Hugo. 90 92 08 50. The atmosphere is
almost too much with its old canvases and palettes
and original counters.

SAINT-TROPEZ - *(Var)*

CAFÉ DES ARTS
Place des Lices. 94 97 02 25. Under the
plane trees close to the *boules* alley,
with its old walls full of memories of
famous painters.

TOULOUSE - *(Haute-Garonne)*

LE CAFÉ BIBENT
5 Place du Capitole. 61 23 89 03. 1870
décor with Moors, goats and pink marble.
In the prettiest square in town.

MUSEUM

At Lignerolles/Saint André de l'Eure in northern
France (in the *departement* of Eure*)* there is a
museum, dedicated to the French grocer's shop*,* with
a reconstruction of a café-épicerie. Open Sundays,
June–September, (tel. 33 25 91 07).

LISTED BUILDINGS

No work may be carried out on 'classified' building
without the permission of the Ministry of Culture
which will then survey it and may contribute 20-80%
of the costs. A 'listed' building may not have work
done on it without informing the Ministry, which
cannot object unless it classifies it. It may not be
destroyed without the permission of the Minister.
The State may not contribute more than 40%.
There is an architect of French Buildings in each
département of France, who directs all work on
classified buildings.

Anyone may write to the Direction Régionale des
Affaires Culturelles (DRAC) of the relevant region
with information on a café which deserves to be
listed or classified .

La Direction du Patrimoine (The Directorate of the
National Heritage), 3 Rue de Valois, 75001 Paris
(tel. 40 15 80 00) can provide addresses of the
appropriate DRAC.

CAFÉ SHOPPING

Increasingly, cafés are displaying and selling plates
and cups, even tables and chairs, that are exactly
the same as those in daily use in their own
establishments. Examples are the Bar du Clown,
the Café Costes, Les Deux Magots, the Flore.

The illustrations in this Guide and on pages 18 and 19 come from an old catalogue of Etablissements A.Berc of Paris.